NIST HANDBOOK 150-2B

National
Voluntary
Laboratory
Accreditation
Program

Calibration Laboratories

Technical Guide for Electromagnetic RF Microwave Measurements

C. Douglas Faison and
Carroll S. Brickenkamp, Editors

February 2004

U.S. Department of Commerce
Donald L. Evans, Secretary

Technology Administration
Phillip J. Bond, Under Secretary for Technology

National Institute of Standards and Technology
Arden L. Bement, Jr., Director

NVLAP AND THE NVLAP LOGO

The term *NVLAP* (represented by the NVLAP logo) is a federally registered certification mark of the National Institute of Standards and Technology and the federal government, who retain exclusive rights to control the use thereof. Permission to use the term and/or logo is granted to NVLAP-accredited laboratories for the limited purposes of announcing their accredited status, and for use on reports that describe only testing and calibration within the scope of accreditation. NIST reserves the right to control the quality of the use of the term *NVLAP* and of the logo itself.

Contents

Preface

The Calibration Laboratories Accreditation Program was developed by the National Voluntary Laboratory Accreditation Program (NVLAP) at the National Institute of Standards and Technology (NIST) as a result of interest from private industry and at the request of the National Conference of Standards Laboratories (now the NCSL International). The goal of the program is to provide a means by which calibration laboratories can be assessed for competency. This voluntary program is not designed to serve as a means of imposing specific calibration procedures or minimum uncertainties on applicant laboratories; instead, the program allows for all scientifically valid calibration schemes and requires that laboratories derive and document their measurement uncertainties.

To accomplish this goal, NVLAP employs technical experts on a contract basis, to serve as assessors in each of the following eight fields of physical metrology calibration:

- electromagnetic dc/low frequency,
- electromagnetic rf/microwave frequency,
- time and frequency,
- ionizing radiation,
- optical radiation,
- dimensional,
- mechanical, and
- thermodynamics.

NIST Handbooks 150-2A through 150-2H are technical guides for the accreditation of calibration laboratories, with each handbook corresponding to one of the eight fields of physical metrology calibration. They are intended for information and use by:

- NVLAP technical experts in assessing laboratories,
- staff of accredited laboratories,
- those laboratories seeking accreditation,
- other laboratory accreditation systems,
- users of laboratory services, and
- others needing information on the requirements and guidelines for accreditation under the NVLAP Calibration Laboratories Accreditation Program.

NOTE   The Calibration Laboratories Accreditation Program has been expanded to cover chemical calibration for the providers of proficiency testing and certifiers of spectrophotometric NTRMs. (See NIST Handbooks 150-19 and 150-21.) Other NVLAP handbooks in the chemical calibration area are expected in the future.

The assessor uses NIST Handbook 150, *NVLAP Procedures and General Requirements*, and the appropriate guides (NIST Handbooks 150-2A through 150-2H) to validate that a laboratory is capable of performing calibrations within the laboratory's stated uncertainties. These technical guides and other relevant technical information support assessors in their assessments of laboratories. Along with inspecting the facilities, documentation, equipment, and personnel, the assessor can witness a calibration, have an item recalibrated, and/or examine the results of measurement assurance programs and round-robins to collect objective evidence.

NIST Handbooks 150-2A through 150-2H supplement NIST Handbook 150, which contains Title 15 of the U.S. Code of Federal Regulations (CFR) Part 285 plus all general NVLAP procedures, criteria, and policies. The criteria in NIST Handbook 150 originally encompassed the requirements of ISO/IEC Guide 25:1990 and the relevant requirements of ISO 9002 (ANSI/ASQC Q92-1987). These handbook criteria have been updated to incorporate the requirements of ISO/IEC 17025:1999.   The entire series of Handbooks 150-2A through

150-2H comprises information specific to the Calibration Laboratories Program and neither adds to nor detracts from requirements contained in NIST Handbook 150.

Any questions or comments on this handbook should be submitted to the National Voluntary Laboratory Accreditation Program, National Institute of Standards and Technology, 100 Bureau Drive, Stop 2140, Gaithersburg, MD 20899-2140; phone (301) 975-4016; fax (301) 926-2884; e-mail NVLAP@nist.gov.

Acknowledgments

NIST Handbook 150-2 was first available as a draft covering all eight fields of physical metrology calibration in one volume. It has been separated into eight handbooks to allow easier updating and electronic downloading from the NVLAP web site. The preparation of these documents has been a joint effort, with input from representatives of other government agencies, laboratories, and the private sector. Acknowledgment of their efforts is in order; however, the listing of individual names is impractical. The submissions by individuals and companies offering suggestions for improvement to this document were also very welcome, as were the contributions of those who attended the public workshops.

We thank all the NIST measurement divisions for their work in writing or contributing to the individual handbooks. Listed below are those from the NIST measurement divisions who deserve special thanks for input to Handbook 150-2B, *Technical Guide for Electromagnetic RF Microwave Measurements*:

- Mr. James Randa and Mr. Wade J. Allen (Thermal Noise),
- Mr. Michael H. Francis (Planar Near-Field Range Antennae),
- Mr. George Free (High Frequency Impedance),
- Mr. Jeffrey A. Jargon and Mr. Ron Ginley (30 MHz Attenuation),
- Mr. John R. Juroshek (Coaxial and Waveguide Devices),
- Mr. George Free and Mr. Gregorio Rebuldela (RF-DC Thermal Voltage Converters and RF-DC Micropotentiometers), and
- Mr. John R. Juroshek, Mr. Ron Ginley, and Mr. Manly P. Weidman (RF/Microwave Power).

Additional thanks go to those who actively participated in the Technical Guide Workshop held November 1993 and to those who served as points of contact within fields of calibration. They include: Ms. Georgia L. Harris, Mr. Norman B. Belecki, Dr. Theodore D. Doiron, Mr. Robert M. Judish, Mr. Thomas C. Larason, Ms. Sally S. Bruce, and Dr. Donald B. Sullivan. A special thanks is owed to Mr. James L. Cigler for work in developing the content and format of this guide, and to Ms. Vanda White for her editorial expertise in making this a readable document.

Above all, we wish to thank Mr. Jon M. Crickenberger, the editor of the first three drafts of this document, for literally hundreds of hours of his work in creating this guide. It was he who tasked the contributors to produce the technical content, assembled the results of their efforts into a consistent format, and provided the general commentary. Without Jon's dedicated effort to this monumental task, this guide would never have been published.

NVLAP has edited the individual handbooks and made changes resulting from comments by individuals to earlier draft versions. This editing has been to a different extent for each parameter. Every effort was made to include all pertinent information relevant to an ISO/IEC 17025-derived technical guide.

C. Douglas Faison and Carroll S. Brickenkamp, Editors
National Voluntary Laboratory Accreditation Program
National Institute of Standards and Technology
100 Bureau Drive, Stop 2140
Gaithersburg, MD 20899-2140

Summary

This guide presents the general technical requirements (i.e., on-site assessment and proficiency testing) of the laboratory accreditation program for calibration laboratories along with specific technical criteria and guidance applicable to rf/microwave measurements. These technical guidelines are presented to indicate how the NVLAP criteria may be applied.

Any calibration laboratory (including commercial, manufacturer, university, or federal, state, or local government laboratory) engaged in calibration in rf/microwave measurements listed in this handbook may apply for NVLAP accreditation. Accreditation will be granted to a laboratory that complies with the criteria for accreditation as defined in NIST Handbook 150. Accreditation does not guarantee laboratory performance – it is a finding of laboratory competence.

Fields of calibration covered: Specific calibration parameters and related stimulus and measurement devices in areas of electromagnetic rf/microwave measurement.

Scope of accreditation:
- Calibration parameter(s), range, and uncertainty level
- Types of measuring and test equipment
- Quality assurance system for measuring and test equipment

Period of accreditation: One year, renewable annually.

On-site assessment: Visit by an assessor(s) to determine compliance with the NVLAP criteria before initial accreditation, in the first renewal year, and every two years thereafter. Preassessment and monitoring visits are conducted as required. All calibration parameters or general areas of calibration within the specific scope of accreditation requested will be assessed.

Assessors: Selected from technical experts with experience in the appropriate areas of calibration and quality systems assessment.

Proficiency testing (measurement assurance): Each laboratory is required to demonstrate its capability to successfully perform calibrations as part of on-site assessment or by documented successful completion of an approved Measurement Assurance Program (MAP) or laboratory intercomparison. Proficiency testing may be required for initial accreditation, or where other evidence of measurement assurance is not evident, and may be conducted annually thereafter. Advance notice and instructions are given before proficiency testing is scheduled.

Fees: Payments are required as listed on the NVLAP fee schedule, including the initial application fee, administrative/technical support fee, on-site assessment fee, and proficiency testing fee.

1 General information

1.1 Purpose

The purpose of this handbook is to amplify the general requirements for accreditation by NVLAP of calibration laboratories in the area of rf/microwave measurements covered by the Calibration Laboratories Program. It complements and supplements the NVLAP programmatic procedures and general requirements found in NIST Handbook 150, *NVLAP Procedures and General Requirements*. The interpretive comments and additional guidelines contained in this handbook make the general NVLAP criteria specifically applicable to the Calibration Laboratories Program.

This handbook does not contain the general requirements for accreditation, which are listed in NIST Handbook 150, but rather provides guidelines for good calibration laboratory practices, which may be useful in achieving accreditation.

1.2 Organization of handbook

The handbook is organized in two sections. The first section provides additional explanations to the general procedures and requirements contained in NIST Handbook 150. The second section provides details and guidance very specific for rf/microwave calibration laboratories.

1.3 Description of Calibration Laboratories Accreditation Program

On May 18, 1992, as a result of the petition and public notice process, the Director of the National Institute of Standards and Technology published in the *Federal Register* a notice of intent to develop the Calibration Laboratories Accreditation Program under the procedures of the National Voluntary Laboratory Accreditation Program. On June 2, 1994, the procedures and general requirements under which NVLAP operates, Title 15, Part 285 of the U.S. Code of Federal Regulations (CFR), were revised to:

a) expand the procedures beyond testing laboratories to include accreditation of calibration laboratories,

b) update the procedures to ensure compatibility with generally accepted conformity assurance and conformity assessment concepts,

c) incorporate international standards changes, especially with relevant International Organization for Standardization/International Electrotechnical Commission (ISO/IEC) documents (e.g., ISO/IEC Guides 25 (now ISO/IEC 17025:1999), 38, 43, and 58, and the ISO 9000 series), and

d) facilitate and promote acceptance of the calibration and test results between countries to avoid barriers to trade.

Calibration laboratory accreditation is offered in eight fields of physical metrology calibration covering a wide variety of parameters and includes accreditation in multifunction measuring and test equipment calibrations. Specific requirements and criteria have been established for determining laboratory qualifications for accreditation following prescribed NVLAP procedures. The criteria address the laboratory's management organization, quality system, personnel, methods and method validation, equipment, control of environmental effects, measurement traceability, sampling methods, handling of test and calibration items, methods to assure the quality of its measurement results, reports, service to its clients, review of requests and contracts, subcontracting, purchasing, control of nonconforming work, handling of complaints, document and record control, corrective and preventive actions, internal audits, and management reviews.

On September 18, 1992, a public workshop was held at NIST Gaithersburg and attended by a mix of private sector and government personnel. The workshop reviewed a draft handbook, which included general requirements, as well as very specific technical requirements for dc voltage calibrations at all levels. As a result of the workshop, the draft handbook was revised to take the form of a Calibration Laboratories Program Handbook, which included the general requirements for laboratories (using ISO/IEC Guide 25 as a basis), and eight companion Technical Guides covering the specific requirements for each field of calibration offered for accreditation.

On May 18, 1993, a public workshop on the revised draft program handbook was held at NIST Boulder and attended by more than 60 industry and government personnel. Comments from this workshop, as well as responses to a survey/checklist mailing, were used to prepare the final draft of the handbook, titled *NVLAP Procedures and General Requirements* (NIST Handbook 150), published in March 1994. NIST Handbook 150 has since been revised to incorporate ISO/IEC 17025.

A public workshop for the Calibration Laboratories Technical Guides was held at NIST Gaithersburg, on November 22 through 24, 1993. More than 60 industry and government personnel attended and provided comments on the draft version of the Technical Guide for each of eight fields of calibration. As a result, the eight Technical Guides were incorporated into a draft Handbook 150-2, *Calibration Laboratories Technical Guide*, covering the fields being offered for accreditation. [In 2000, Handbook 150-2 (draft) was divided into eight handbooks, 150-2A through 150-2H, one for each calibration area.]

The need for technical experts to serve as assessors was advertised, and the first group of assessors was selected and trained during a four-day session held from November 16 through 19, 1993, in Gaithersburg, using materials developed by NVLAP.

The Calibration Laboratories Accreditation Program officially began accepting applications when notification was given in the *Federal Register* dated May 11, 1994. Applications are accepted and processed following procedures found in NIST Handbook 150.

1.4 References

1.4.1   The following documents are referenced in this handbook.

a)   NIST Handbook 150, *NVLAP Procedures and General Requirements*; available from:

> National Voluntary Laboratory Accreditation Program
> National Institute of Standards and Technology
> 100 Bureau Drive, Stop 2140
> Gaithersburg, MD 20899-2140
>
> Phone: (301) 975-4016
> Fax: (301) 926-2884
> E-mail: nvlap@nist.gov
> NVLAP Web site: http://www.nist.gov/nvlap

b)   ISO/IEC/BIPM (BIPM is the Bureau International des Poids et Mesures, the International Bureau of Weights and Measures) *Guide to the Expression of Uncertainty in Measurement* (GUM), 1993.

c)   ISO/IEC 17025: 1999: *General requirements for the competence of testing and calibration laboratories.*

d)   ISO/IEC Guide 43: 1997, *Proficiency testing by interlaboratory comparisons, Part 1 and Part 2.*

e)   ISO/IEC/BIPM *International Vocabulary of Basic and General Terms in Metrology* (VIM), 1993.

ISO documents b) through e) are available from:

Global Engineering Documents (paper copies)
Order phone: (800) 854-7179

American National Standards Institute (ANSI) (electronic copies)
Electronic Standards Store
ANSI web site: http://www.ansi.org

f)   ANSI/IEEE Std. 100-1996, *IEEE Standard Dictionary of Electrical & Electronics Terms.*

g)   Taylor, Barry N., and Chris E. Kuyatt, *Guidelines for Evaluating and Expressing the Uncertainty of NIST Measurement Results*, NIST Technical Note 1297, U.S. Government Printing Office, Washington DC, 1994. Available on-line at http://physics.nist.gov/Document/tn1297.pdf.

h)   NCSL International Recommended Practice RP-15: *Guide for Interlaboratory Comparisons*, 1999.

i)   ANSI/NCSL Z540-1-1994, *Calibration Laboratories and Measuring and Test Equipment—General Requirements.*

j)   NCSL International Recommended Practice RP-7: *Laboratory Design*, 1993.

NCSL International documents h) through j) are available from:

NCSL International
2995 Wilderness Place, Suite 107
Boulder, CO 80301-5404
Phone: (303) 440-3339
Fax: (303) 440-3384
E-mail: orders@ncsli.org
Web site: http://www.ncsli.org

k)   Ehrlich, C. D., and S. D. Rasberry, "Metrological Timelines in Traceability," *J. Res. Natl. Inst. Stand. Technol.* **103**, 93 (1998).

l)   Croarkin, M. C., Measurement Assurance Programs, Part II: Development and Implementation, *NBS Special Publication 676-II*, U.S. Government Printing Office, Washington, DC, 1985.

1.4.2   Additional references specific to electromagnetic rf/microwave measurements are listed in Sections 2.3 through 2.9.

1.5 Definitions

Definitions found in NIST Handbook 150 apply, but may be interpreted differently or stated differently, when necessary to amplify or clarify the meaning of specific words or phrases as they apply to specific technical criteria.

1.5.1   Ac-dc transfer principle: A dc voltage is substituted for the ac voltage to be measured. The dc is adjusted to give the same output emf from the thermocouple as that obtained with the ac applied. This is measured with a suitable measuring device.

1.5.2   Continuous wave: A wave whose successive oscillations are identical under steady-state conditions.

1.5.3   Direct substitution: The act of substituting one quantity or signal source for another. Typically a dc current or voltage is substituted for an ac or rf current or voltage.

1.5.4   Lindeck potentiometer: A potentiometer in which an unknown potential difference is balanced against a known potential difference derived from a fixed resistance carrying a variable current.

1.5.5   Micropotentiometer: A source of voltage potential drop across a known resistance, through which currents flow. These resistances are of the order of $m\Omega$ (for μV levels), and therefore constitute an essentially zero source impedance (constant voltage source).

1.5.6   National reference standard: A set of thermal voltage converters maintained by the national measurement laboratory against which other converters are compared.

1.5.7   Precision (of a measurement process): The quality of coherence or repeatability of measurement data; the similarity of successive independent measurements of a single magnitude generated by repeated applications of the process under specified conditions.

1.5.8   Proficiency testing: Determination of laboratory performance by means of comparing and evaluating calibrations or tests on the same or similar items or materials by two or more laboratories in accordance with predetermined conditions. For the NVLAP Calibration Laboratories Accreditation Program, this entails using a transport standard as a measurement artifact, sending it to applicant laboratories to be measured, and then comparing the applicant laboratory's results to those of a reference laboratory on the same artifact.

1.5.9   Quality assurance: A system of activities, the purpose of which is to provide to the producer or user the assurance that the product or service meets defined standards of quality with a stated level of confidence.

1.5.10   Quality control: A system of activities, the purpose of which is to control the quality of a product or service such that it is satisfactory, adequate, dependable and economic.

1.5.11   Random error: The error equal to error minus systematic error; because only a finite number of measurements can be made, it is only possible to determine an estimate of random error.

1.5.12   Rf-dc difference (thermal voltage converters – TVC or micropotentiometer – μPOT): The difference, usually expressed in percent, between the rf and dc input voltages required to produce an identical dc output voltage from the thermocouple used as a current indicating device within the thermal transfer device.

1.5.13   Systematic uncertainty: The inherent offset of a measurement process or one of its components; the difference between the true value and the mean value obtained in a measurement system in a stable environment.

1.5.14 Thermal voltage converter: A thermoelement rated for low current input and associated with a series resistor, such that the emf developed at the output terminals gives a reliable measure of the voltage applied to the input terminals.

1.5.15 Thermoelement: The simplest type of thermal converter, consisting of a heater and thermocouple. In its usual form, the heater is a short, straight wire suspended between two supporting wires in an evacuated glass envelope; the hot junction of the thermocouple is fastened to the midpoint of the heater and is electrically insulated from it with a small bead.

1.5.16 Total uncertainty: The sum of the estimated systematic uncertainty and random uncertainties attributed to the imprecision of the measurement process.

1.5.17 Traceability: Property of the result of a measurement or the value of a standard whereby it can be related to stated references, usually national or international standards, through an unbroken chain of comparisons all having stated uncertainties. [VIM:1993, 6.10]

A single measurement intercomparison is sufficient to establish uncertainty relationships only over a limited time interval (see reference 1.4.1 k)); internal measurement assurance (see reference 1.4.1 l)), using control (check) standards, is required to fully demonstrate that uncertainties remain within stated levels over time. For the purposes of demonstrating traceability for NVLAP accreditation, a laboratory must demonstrate not only that there is an unbroken chain of comparisons to national standards, but also that this chain is supported by appropriate uncertainties, measurement assurance processes, continuous standards maintenance, proper calibration procedures, and proper handling of standards. In this way, traceability is related to these other areas of calibration.

1.5.18 Transfer standard: An artifact standard that is used to transfer calibration information from one standards laboratory to another.

1.6 NVLAP documentation

1.6.1 Accreditation documents

Laboratories granted NVLAP accreditation are provided with two documents: Scope of Accreditation and Certificate of Accreditation.

The Scope of Accreditation lists the "Best Uncertainty" that an accredited laboratory can provide for a given range or nominal value within a given parameter of measurement. This "Best Uncertainty" is a statement of the smallest uncertainty that a laboratory has been assessed as capable of providing for that particular range or nominal value. The actual reported value of uncertainty for any particular measurement service that the accredited laboratory provides under its scope may vary depending on such contributors as the statistics of the test and uncertainties associated with the device under test.

1.6.2 Fields of calibration/parameters selection list

The Calibration Laboratories program encompasses eight fields of physical metrology calibration, with multiple parameters under each field. Each field is covered by a separate handbook (NIST Handbooks 150-2A through 150-2H). (Fields of accreditation under Chemical Calibration are covered by separate handbooks.) Depending on the extent of its calibration capabilities, a laboratory may seek accreditation in all or only selected fields and parameters within the scope of the program. The fields of calibration and their related parameters are given on the Fields of Calibration and Parameters Selection List, which is provided to a laboratory seeking accreditation as part of the NVLAP application package for the program. Additional fields of calibration and/or parameters may be added to the Calibration Laboratories program upon request of customer laboratories and/or if decided by NVLAP to be in the best interest of the Calibration Laboratories Program.

The laboratory is requested to indicate on the Fields of Calibration/Parameters Selection List the parameter(s) for which accreditation is desired, along with appropriate ranges and uncertainties. There is also provision for an applicant laboratory to request accreditation for parameters not currently listed on the Selection List, or for accreditation of the quality system employed for assuring Measurement and Test Equipment (M & TE) used in support of product certification. Request for accreditation of quality assurance systems for M & TE will be treated as a separate field of calibration for the purpose of setting appropriate fees. Once a laboratory meets all the requirements for accreditation for the Fields of Calibration/Parameters Selection List, this information will become the basis for the Scope of Accreditation document.

1.6.3 Checklists

Checklists enable assessors to document the assessment of the laboratory against the NVLAP requirements found in NIST Handbook 150. The NVLAP Calibration Laboratories Accreditation Program incorporates the NVLAP General Operations Checklist. The questions are applicable to evaluating a laboratory's ability to operate a calibration program, and address factors such as the laboratory's organization, management, and quality system in addition to its calibration competency.

The NVLAP General Operations Checklist is numbered to correspond to the requirements in NIST Handbook 150. Comment sheets are used by the assessor to explain deficiencies noted on the checklist. Additionally, the assessor may use the sheets to make comments on aspects of the laboratory's performance other than deficiencies.

1.7 Assessing and evaluating a laboratory

1.7.1 On-site assessment

1.7.1.1 The NVLAP lead assessor will schedule with the laboratory the date for on-site evaluation, and will request the quality manual and documented quality and calibration procedures in advance of the visit to reduce time spent at the laboratory; such materials will be returned by the assessor. NVLAP and the assessor will protect the confidentiality of the materials and information provided. The laboratory should be prepared to conduct routine calibrations, have equipment in good working order, and be ready for examination according to the guidance contained in this handbook, the requirements identified in NIST Handbook 150, and the laboratory's quality manual. The assessor will need time and work space to complete assessment documentation while at the laboratory, and will discuss these needs at the opening meeting of the on-site assessment.

1.7.1.2 NVLAP technical assessors are provided with the NVLAP General Operations Checklist to help ensure the completeness, objectivity, and uniformity of the on-site assessment.

1.7.1.3 When accreditation has been requested for a considerable number of fields of calibration and parameters, the assessment may range from observing calibrations in progress, requiring repeat measurements on completed calibrations, to listening to laboratory staff describe the calibration process. The depth into which the assessor performs the assessment depends on the number of fields of calibration and associated parameters for which accreditation is requested and the time required to perform a given calibration.

1.7.1.4   The assessor, or the assessment team, does the following during a typical on-site assessment:

a)   Conducts an entry briefing with the laboratory manager to explain the purpose of the on-site visit and to discuss the schedule for the day(s). At the discretion of the laboratory manager, other staff may attend the briefing.

b)   Reviews quality system manual, equipment and maintenance records, record-keeping procedures, laboratory calibration reports, and personnel competency records. At least one laboratory staff member must be available to answer questions; however, the assessor may wish to review the documents alone. The assessor(s) does not usually ask to take any laboratory documents with him/her, and previously supplied documents will be returned.

c)   Physically examines equipment and facilities, observes the demonstration of selected procedures by appropriate personnel assigned to perform calibrations, and interviews the personnel.   The demonstrations must include preparation for calibration of devices, and the setup and use of measuring and test equipment, standards and systems.

d)   Holds an exit briefing with the laboratory manager and staff to discuss the assessment findings. Deficiencies are discussed and resolutions may be mutually agreed upon. Items that must be addressed before accreditation can be granted are emphasized; outstanding deficiencies require response to NVLAP within 30 days. Items that have been corrected during the on-site and any recommendations are specially noted.

e)   Completes an On-site Assessment Report, as part of the exit briefing, summarizing the findings. The assessor(s) attaches copies of the completed checklists to this report during the exit briefing. The report is signed by the lead assessor and the laboratory's Authorized Representative to acknowledge the discussion. This signature does not necessarily indicate agreement; challenge(s) may be made through NVLAP. A copy is given to the representative for retention. All observations made by the NVLAP assessor are held in the strictest confidence.

1.7.2   Proficiency testing

1.7.2.1   Background

Once the quality system review and on-site assessment steps have been satisfactorily completed, it is necessary to gather another set of data points to aid in deciding whether or not the applicant laboratory is competent to perform calibrations within the fields of interest to the uncertainties claimed. In the eight fields of calibration covered by Handbooks 150-2A through 150-2H, there are approximately 85 parameters of interest. Under most parameters there are several subsets, referred to as ranges. For example, coaxial fixed and variable attenuators with many different types of connectors can be measured over frequency ranges from 10 MHz to 50 GHz. In view of the many possible ranges (and in this case, connectors), proficiency testing could be conducted in hundreds of areas. NVLAP reserves the right to test by sampling in any area; hence, applicant laboratories must be prepared, with reasonable notice, to demonstrate proficiency in any of a number of parameters.

1.7.2.2   Proficiency testing vs. measurement assurance

There is an important difference between proficiency testing and measurement assurance. The objective of proficiency testing is to determine through a measurement process that the laboratory's measurement results compare favorably with the measurement results of the audit laboratory (NIST or one designated by NVLAP), taking into account the relative uncertainties assigned by both the applicant and audit laboratories. The objective of proficiency testing is not to determine and certify the total uncertainty of the applicant laboratory, as is done in a Measurement Assurance Program (MAP) with NIST, but to verify (through the assessment process) that the uncertainty claimed by the applicant laboratory is reasonable, and then use the claimed uncertainty to test that the measurement result obtained through the proficiency test is acceptable.

It is neither the intention nor the mission of NVLAP to conduct MAPs or to otherwise provide traceability for laboratories. Laboratories obtain these services from the NIST measurement divisions. NVLAP assesses the implementation, application, and documentation of MAPs by laboratories. NVLAP accreditation encourages the use of MAPs by the calibration laboratory community, and MAP results produce objective evidence that NVLAP assessors look for as part of the assessment process.

1.7.2.3   Requirements

NVLAP's proficiency testing program uses a sampling approach. All applicant laboratories are required to complete an annual proficiency test in one parameter under each field of calibration for which it has applied to be accredited. For the purposes of the NVLAP Calibration Laboratories Accreditation Program, the results of the proficiency test are considered as objective evidence, along with the on-site visit, of a laboratory's ability to perform competent calibrations. Proficiency testing is conducted annually using different parameters in each field; however, those laboratories accredited in only one parameter within a field are retested in the same parameter.

1.7.2.4   Uncertainty determination

The applicant laboratory is required to perform a measurement or series of measurements on an artifact using the same calibration method, apparatus, and personnel that it uses to calibrate its customers' equipment. The laboratory must be able to identify and quantify all sources of uncertainty that affect the measurement. The laboratory should attach an overall uncertainty to the measurement by combining all uncertainty contributions, in their type A and type B components, in the root-sum-squared method as described in the *Guide to the Expression of Uncertainty in Measurement*. The confidence limit used should be k = 2, which is equivalent to a 95% confidence probability.

1.7.2.5   Pass/fail criteria

The performance of the proficiency test is judged by calculating the error of the measurement, normalized with respect to the uncertainty of the measurement, using the following equation:

$$E_{normal} = \left| \left(Value_{lab} - Value_{ref}\right) / \left(Uncertainty_{ref}^2 + Uncertainty_{lab}^2\right)^{1/2} \right|$$

where

E_{normal} = normalized error of the applicant laboratory
$Value_{lab}$ = the value as measured by the applicant laboratory
$Value_{ref}$ = the value as measured by the reference laboratory
$Uncertainty_{ref}$ = the uncertainty of the reference laboratory
$Uncertainty_{lab}$ = the uncertainty of the applicant laboratory

To pass the proficiency test, the applicant laboratory must have a value for E_{normal} less than 1 (i.e., $E_{normal} < 1$). The results may be plotted graphically, with lines representing the limits of uncertainty of the measurements. The anonymity of each applicant laboratory will always be preserved.

1.7.2.6 Scheduling and handling

Proficiency testing is scheduled by NVLAP-designated reference laboratories. These sites are NIST laboratories or NVLAP-accredited laboratories that have been found to have the ability to perform the required proficiency tests to an uncertainty level appropriate for the laboratories they evaluate. The proficiency test is scheduled independently and not to correspond with the on-site visit. Applicant laboratories are notified in advance as to the approximate arrival time of the measurement artifact. Instructions for performing the test, reporting the results, communicating with the reference laboratory, and shipping are included along with the artifact as part of the proficiency test package. Applicant laboratories are instructed to perform all required measurements within a reasonable time and are told where to ship the artifacts once the testing has been completed.

1.7.2.7 Notification of results

NVLAP notifies each laboratory of its own results in a proficiency test. If a laboratory has received its on-site assessment prior to the completion of the proficiency test, the status of that laboratory's accreditation is contingent upon successful completion of proficiency testing. The laboratory's accreditation status may be changed to reflect a partial accreditation, or may be completely suspended pending demonstration of the laboratory's ability to successfully complete the proficiency test at a later date.

1.7.3 Traceability

1.7.3.1 Establishing traceability

Laboratories must establish an unbroken chain of comparisons leading to the appropriate international or national standard, such that the uncertainties of the comparisons support the level of uncertainty that the laboratory gives to its customers. Generally speaking, the uncertainties of the comparisons increase as they move from a higher (international or national level) to a lower level standard. This uncertainty chain is the evidence of traceability and must be documented accordingly. Traceability does not simply mean having standards calibrated at the national laboratory, but must consider how a measurement, with its corresponding uncertainty, is transferred from the national level to the calibration laboratory's customers.

1.7.3.2 Considerations in determining traceability

Without some type of continuous measurement assurance process, one cannot be reasonably certain that the comparisons have been transferred properly to the laboratory's customers. The measurement process itself must be verified to be in control over time. Therefore, traceability is not a static concept that, once established, may be ignored; it is dynamic. Process control exercised in each calibration provides the assurance that a valid transfer of the international or national standard has taken place. This assurance may be accomplished through the use of tools such as check standards and control charts. Also, the laboratory's primary standards must be maintained in such a way as to verify their integrity. Examples of this may be having more than one primary standard to use for intercomparisons, monitoring the primary standard with a check or working standard (looking for changes), and verifying a primary standard on a well-characterized measurement/calibration system. Using scientifically sound measurement procedures to transfer the primary standard value to the working level and the customer's item is essential to establishing traceability. If the procedure itself yields the wrong result, there is no way the laboratory can perform a calibration traceable to the international or national standard. Handling the laboratory's standards affects the measurement process, and therefore the ability to transfer the standard's value to the customer. Examples of handling problems are dirty or improperly cleaned standards, maintaining standards in an improper environment, not maintaining custody and security of the standards or the items under test, and improper handling of standards or test items during the measurement process.

1.7.3.3   Relationship to existing standards

The above discussion illustrates how traceability is dependent on many aspects of the measurement process and therefore must be considered in all phases of calibration. It is not just coincidental that the factors addressed above are main topics of concern in ISO/IEC 17025:1999.

1.7.4   Uncertainty

NVLAP recognizes the methodology for determining uncertainty as described in the *Guide to the Expression of Uncertainty in Measurement*, published by ISO. To be NVLAP-accredited, a laboratory must document the derivation of the uncertainties that it reports to its customers. These uncertainties will appear on the scope issued to each accredited laboratory to an accuracy appropriate to the standards, procedures, and measuring devices used.

2 Criteria for accreditation

2.1 Introduction

2.1.1 Applicant laboratories are assessed using the requirements in NIST Handbook 150, *NVLAP Procedures and General Requirements*. This guide, NIST Handbook 150-2B, was developed from a NIST measurement laboratory perspective and provides examples and guidelines, not requirements, to assessors and interested calibration laboratories, on good laboratory practices and recommended standards. Therefore, the guide language reflects this philosophy through the use of "shoulds" instead of "shalls" (along with other less prescriptive language) when describing criteria. The requirements presented here are not absolute since specific requirements depend on the measurement uncertainty for which an applicant laboratory wishes to be accredited. This is a business decision for each laboratory and beyond the scope of NVLAP. Simply stated, to be accredited, an applicant laboratory must have a quality system and be able to prove (and document) that it is capable of doing what it says it does (i.e., correctly calibrate to a stated uncertainty) within the framework of NIST Handbook 150. Accreditation will be granted, and therefore may be referenced in calibration reports, etc., only for those specific parameters, ranges and uncertainties using calibration methods and procedures for which a laboratory has been evaluated. Calibrations performed by a laboratory using methods and procedures not considered appropriate for the level of measurements being made, and which have not been evaluated by the accreditation process, are outside the scope of accreditation and may not be referenced as "accredited" calibrations on calibration reports, etc.

2.1.2 Section 2.2 describes areas of commonality among all rf/microwave parameters, and sections 2.3 through 2.10 provide specific calibration guidelines for rf/microwave measurements and references to related standards and documents. This guide is dynamic in that new parameters may be added and existing criteria updated and improved.

2.2 Areas of commonality among all rf/microwave parameters

2.2.1 Introduction

Electromagnetic measurements in the rf/microwave region have developed over a much shorter time span than the classical low frequency measurements. This field of measurement technology is still evolving and broadening its horizons. In low frequency electrical measurements, the parameters measured are derived from lumped parameter ac circuit theory while in the rf/microwave region both lumped parameter circuit theory and transmission line theory are used to arrive at the parameters. Thus in some cases, at rf/microwave frequencies, measurements can be traced to specific standards that are absolute measurements of the parameter, i.e., capacitance measurements, while at other times the measurements are relative, i.e., the measurement of attenuation. Due to evolving measurement techniques and the minimal number of parameters that are well-characterized through traceability to national standards, it is often difficult in the rf/microwave region of measurement to define what measurement methodology should be used or the uncertainties to which a measurement should be achievable.

2.2.2 Scope

This section discusses the specific technical criteria for rf/microwave electromagnetic measurement in the following areas:

a)   High frequency impedence,

b)   Rf/microwave power (thermister mounts and power detectors),

---

c) Planar near-field range antenna calibration,

d) Thermal noise measurements,

e) Microwave measurements of scattering parameters,

f) 30-MHz attenuation measurements,

g) Rf-dc thermal converter measurements, and

h) Rf-dc micropotentiometer measurements.

2.2.3 Estimation of uncertainty of measurement

2.2.3.1 Calibration laboratory measurements are useful only if quantitative and thoroughly documented statements of uncertainty accompany them. The uncertainty of measurements on a microwave system, like most other systems, consists of several components. These components can usually be grouped into the following two categories:

a) those which are evaluated by statistical methods; and

b) those which are evaluated by other means.

2.2.3.2 The classification of uncertainty components into these categories is often not simple. A "random" component may become a "systematic" component and vice versa depending on how the system is modeled or how the data is viewed. It is recommended that the calibration laboratory provide a thoroughly documented uncertainty statement in accordance with the recommendations of the International Committee for Weights and Measures (CIPM) (see references 2.7.6. l) and m) as well as 1.4.1 b) and g)).

2.2.4 Assuring the quality of test and calibration results

The laboratory should maintain some form of statistical process control (SPC) commensurate with the accuracy levels needed for the calibration. The SPC parameters should be based on measurements of check standards (or closure parameters) and the repeatability of multiple measurements. The frequency and number of process control checks should be appropriate for the level of uncertainty and reliability claimed for the calibration.

2.2.5 Personnel

Those with technical responsibility for rf/microwave calibrations should have the following:

a) A rudimentary understanding of the basic concepts of statistical analysis and error analysis or access to someone capable of interpreting measurement data.

b) A good understanding of electrical principles and the theory and methodology for specific calibrations for which they are responsible. Specific calibration knowledge could include thermal properties of standards and transfer devices and the interactions that are present with circuits and instrumentation.

c) An understanding of the primary factors that contribute to measurement sensitivity and errors in calibrations for which they are responsible.

2.2.6 Accommodation and environmental conditions

2.2.6.1 The temperature in the calibration laboratory should be maintained at a nominal value of 23 °C. The maximum allowable variation is dependent on the calibration parameter, and should be recorded on a continuous or sampled basis. Records of abnormal environmental conditions should be retained for a period of no less than one year.

2.2.6.2 Environmental factors vary widely for the various measurements listed in 2.2.2. Some measurements must be done outside, (e.g., antenna) while others need a temperature controlled environment (e.g., capacitance). Therefore, this topic will be discussed more completely in specific subsections.

2.2.7 Equipment

In general, the complement of reference standards used to perform calibrations of secondary or working standards or instruments with the stated accuracies should be documented and proven to perform at a level adequate to achieve accuracies for which accreditation is requested. Other combinations of standards may be adequate as well. All equipment selections should be supported by adequate historical data, uncertainty analysis, and statistical process control systems.

2.3 High frequency impedance measurements

2.3.1 Background

The measurement of high frequency impedance is most commonly done with some type of automatic impedance measuring instrument, i.e, LCR meters (inductance capacitance resistance meters). When the highest accuracy is desired, some type of bridge is used. Bridges are usually dedicated to a specific type of measurement and the bridge components are discrete components, e.g., generator, transfer device, and detector. Calibration procedures for the two types of measuring instrumentation (LCR meters and bridges) are quite different. While bridge calibrations are dependent on the calibration of individual components, LCR meters must be calibrated as a total system. Calibration procedures for both types of devices are complicated by the minimal number of standards that are commercially available, the various connector sizes (which necessitates the use of adapters from one connector size to another), and within a specific standard type, the number of connectors for the specific standard, i.e., whether it is a one-, two- or four-port device.

2.3.2 Scope

2.3.2.1 This section discusses the specific technical criteria with which a laboratory should demonstrate that it operates in accordance, if it is to be recognized as competent to carry out calibrations in the area of resistance, capacitance and inductance at rf frequencies.

2.3.2.2 This document may also be used as a guide by calibration laboratories in the development and implementation of their quality systems.

2.3.2.3 This document will treat two distinct types of calibration situations:

a) **Situation 1**: Calibration of standards in circumstances where the ratio between manufacturer's stated accuracy (see definition below) of the standard and that of the reference standard is less than four to one.

b) **Situation 2**: Calibration of standards in circumstances where the ratio between manufacturers' stated accuracy of the standard and that of the reference standard is equal to or greater than four to one.

2.3.2.4   It should be noted that these two situations require different skills and knowledge and therefore demonstrated competence in one may not be sufficient to guarantee adequate performance in the other.

2.3.3   Definitions

2.3.3.1   Adaptor: A coaxial connector whose two ends have different types of connectors.

2.3.3.2   Four-port standard: A standard whose access is through four terminal pairs. Normally, there are two pairs of inner connectors that are shorted together and the two pairs are connected to the ends of the impedance. The outer ones are connected to the shield of the standard.

2.3.3.3   Manufacturer's stated accuracy: Generalized statement or collection of statements describing the qualitative performance of an instrument under very broad conditions. (These statements sometimes contain such terms as "typical" or "nominal" accuracy, where accuracy is a qualitative term.) Such statements are made by the manufacturer for sales or warranty purposes or by the user to facilitate categorizing the instrument within an inventory or making broad statements regarding its suitability for use in making a particular measurement.

NOTE   Use of this terminology does not excuse the laboratory from demonstrating, through uncertainty analysis, that it has adequate measurement capability to perform the measurement needed either to assign values or corrections to standards or to verify the performance of instruments and standards it is responsible for calibrating.

2.3.3.4   One-port standard: A standard whose access is a single terminal pair.

2.3.3.5   Situation 1: When the ratio between manufacturer's stated accuracy of the standard and that of the reference standard is less than four to one.

2.3.3.6   Situation 2: When the ratio between manufacturer's stated accuracy and that of the reference standard is equal to or greater than four to one.

2.3.3.7   Transfer device: The instrumentation used to measure impedance standards.

2.3.3.8   Transport standard: A standard especially designed to be minimally affected by the rigors of transportation or by laboratory influence factors, and to have very predictable behavior over a period of time adequate for the evaluation of one measurement system in terms of another.

2.3.3.9   Two-port standard: A standard whose access is through two terminal pairs. Normally, the inner of the two pairs is connected to the impedance and the outer of the two pairs is connected to the shield of the standard.

2.3.4   Quality system

2.3.4.1   Items specified in this section are minimum requirements for accreditation for the applications noted, and evidence pertaining to each should be available for review.

2.3.4.2   In **situation 1** where reference standards are directly traceable to a national measurement institute's (such as NIST's) standards of resistance, capacitance, or inductance, the general requirements include:

a)   A calibration history of the traceable standard(s) with knowledge of drift rate, and where appropriate, the temperature coefficient of the standard.

b) Documented results of an experiment determining the frequency dependence of the standard, where standards are used at frequencies other then those directly traceable to national standards.

c) Laboratory environmental monitoring with a method of applying corrections, if applicable.

d) Calibration history of the device used to compare unknown standards with reference standards.

    1) Where a characterized system is used in the measurements, tests supporting the validity of the accuracy of the measurement are required as well as tests supporting the linearity of the transfer device within the range that it is used. When the measuring system is used to determine two parameters (magnitude and phase, series resistance and inductance, etc.), documentation should exist for both parameters.

    2) Where bridges and discrete devices are used, a schematic of the bridge circuit with details of connections to the oscillator and detector is needed. Methods used to calibrate the bridge components must be documented. Test history and documentation supporting the calibration of the critical bridge elements, documentation of bridge equations, and the error budget assigned to the various components of the bridge and the total system must be available. A history of the standards used in the calibration of the bridge should also be available.

e) Documentation on the care, storage and handling of the standards.

f) Documentation of the software used to assign values to measured quantities. This documentation should consist of a general flow chart, critical equations used in the calculation, and correction factors that are applied in the calculation.

2.3.4.3 In **situation 2**, the requirements could be met in several ways. Of course, systems that qualify for situation 1 will also qualify for situation 2. Another possibility would be to do as in situation 1, but documentation of those elements that do not contribute significantly to the total error of the system could be ignored as long as the total error budget remains within the desired limits. A third possibility would contain the following elements:

a) A process for maintaining check standards at the values where measurements will be done with documentation of the check standard history.

b) Evaluation of scaling processes where check standards are not available within the tolerance of the calibration.

c) History of the measurements made on the system with the check standards.

2.3.5 Accommodation and environmental conditions

2.3.5.1 The environment of the laboratory should be controlled according to applicable provisions of NCSL International Recommended Practice RP-7 with the exception of relative humidity, which should be a maximum of 55 %. Temperature and relative humidity should be recorded on a continuous or sampled basis. Records of abnormal conditions should be retained for a period to be determined by the laboratory, but no less than one year.

2.3.5.2 The quality of electric mains supplying power for instrumentation should be in compliance with applicable provisions of NCSL International Recommended Practice RP-7. Alternatively, these provisions may be met through the use of uninterruptible power supplies.

2.3.5.3   Electrical and magnetic fields should be controlled to be in compliance with the provisions of NCSL International Recommended Practice RP-7.

2.3.6   Equipment

In general, the complement of reference standards used to perform calibrations of secondary or working standards or instruments with the stated accuracies should be documented and proven to perform at a level adequate to achieve uncertainties for which accreditation is requested. Other combinations of standards may be adequate as well. All equipment selections should be supported by adequate historical data, uncertainty analysis, and statistical process control systems.

2.3.7   Estimation of uncertainty of measurement

2.3.7.1   Situation 1 - For circumstances where measurement uncertainties approaching that of a national measurement institute such as NIST are required, the following areas should be considered:

a)   Traceability should be established for the reference standard through the use of a carefully evaluated transport standard to be calibrated at a national measurement institute (NMI) such as NIST or at a laboratory accredited by NVLAP or another accrediting body with which NVLAP has a mutual recognition arrangement. Except under extraordinary conditions, the reference standard should not be removed from the laboratory and should be maintained at operational environmental conditions continuously to sustain traceability.

b)   After an appropriate data history is accumulated, a statistical model of the behavior of the reference standard should be developed and used to assign its values and their uncertainties. This model should be verified on a regular basis via calibration transfers and by analysis of the behavior of the reference standard, the transport standard, and the check standards from both statistical and metrological points of view.

c)   The history of the reference standards should include a history of calibrations of the reference standard immediately before and after the transport standard is calibrated at either the NMI or selected accredited laboratory. The reference standard should be calibrated following any significant change in the measurement system structure or immediately following any measurement problem revealed by check standard data and not proven to be a problem inherent in the check standard. The transport standards should be recalibrated at the NMI with measurements taken before and after the calibration at the NMI.

2.3.7.2   In **situation 2**, parts a) and b) from **situation 1** may constitute traceability. If check standards are used to maintain the measurement process, then the calibration history of the check standards compared to the laboratory reference standards should be documented.

2.3.8   Test and calibration methods and method validation

2.3.8.1   Measurement methods used should minimize or take into account the following effects at a level of precision sufficient to comply with the requirements of the calibration:

a)   adaptors used in connecting standards,

b)   leakage currents,

c)   electrostatic interference,

d)   electromagnetic interference,

e) instrument offsets and drifts,

f) short-term environmental fluctuations, and

g) physical condition of connectors.

2.3.8.2 There are essentially two approaches to calibrations, depending on the level of uncertainty to which the metrologist is working. These approaches are independent of the physical or parametric characteristics of the test items. The two approaches are:

a) direct intercomparison of standards and unknowns, and

b) measurement of unknowns on a system characterized against standards.

2.3.8.3 Both approaches are described to provide some insight into the process by which an assessor can determine whether or not the approach is valid for any given application, and to assess whether or not uncertainty and its associated traceability have been satisfactorily achieved.

2.3.8.4   Direct comparison

a) Some typical measurement parameters using this approach include resistance (using a current comparator) and capacitance (using a transformer ratio bridge). In this process, the standard and unknown are simultaneously in the measuring circuit and the value of the unknown is determined either directly or indirectly (using correction factors) with respect to the known value of the standard. The degree to which the standard is actually known determines, along with transfer uncertainties arising from the act of measurement, the uncertainty in measurement of the unknown. This technique may result in the achievement of a total measurement uncertainty relatively close to that of the standard being used. This is due to the fact that the laboratory quantifies type A and type B uncertainties through a program of statistical process control. The comparator is maintained in control through the use of control charts, which are analyzed continuously as part of the measurement process.

b) Critical to determining the uncertainties of this process is the understanding of the measurement scheme (multiple standards versus multiple unknowns), the intention of the measurement design to identify or eliminate measurement effects such as left-right effects, and the statistical techniques employed (T and F testing, standard deviation computation, etc.). These technical issues, endorsed by management, should be stated in the quality manual and, if necessary, reiterated in the operational procedures of the respective measurement discipline.

2.3.8.5   Unknowns measured on a characterized system

a) In this technique, a measurement system is characterized either by a systematic determination of the measurement that it produces when measuring a standard or group of standards or by the calibration of specific components of the measurement system and using these calibration values in an equation that models the bridge performance. In the first case, the measurement uncertainty is obtained by analysis of the system performance when measuring a group of standards. In the second case, the uncertainty will be derived from an analysis of the bridge equations and determining the effect of the different calibrated components on the results of a measurement. In both cases the measurement system should be maintained in control through the use of control charts. In some cases where it is determined that there are short-term systematic errors present, they are often "calibrated" or adjusted out so that the system reads correctly when a standard is measured. One should be careful to ensure that the systematic error is quantifiable both in magnitude and phase.

b) Having standardized the measurement system, the unknowns are measured with enough redundant measurements to develop an estimate of random uncertainty, which is added as a type A component to the uncertainty assigned to the measurement system.

c) These systems are usually comprised of several stimulus and measurement components and some may be candidates for individual calibration. Assuming the system is maintained in measurement process control through the use of reference and check standards and appropriate control chart analysis and corrective action, the appropriate components should be identified as either requiring or not requiring periodic calibration.

d) As in the first case, all levels of management should be committed to the chosen method of standardization and uncertainty determination as clearly specified in the quality manual. The manual should be explainable to the assessor and all control charts and other supporting measurement data should be readily available for on-site assessment.

2.3.9 References

a) Field, R. F., Sinclair, D. B., "A method for determining the residual inductance and resistance of a variable air condenser at radio frequencies," *Proceedings of the Institute of Radio Engineers*, **24**, (2), Feb. 1936, pp 255-274.

b) Millea, A., "Connector pair techniques for the accurate measurement of two-terminal low-value capacitances," *Journal of Research of the National Bureau of Standards, C Engineering & Instrumentation*, **74C**, Dec 1970, pp 111-116.

c) Woods, D., *A precision V.H.F. twin-t dual admittance bridge and associated standards*, Aeronautical Inspection Directorate, 1950.

d) Clarke, R. N., *Notes on the use and theory of the XT-90 (Woods) twin-t dual admittance bridge*, Memorandum of Division of Electrical Science, National Physical Laboratory, 1978.

e) Jones, R. N., "Evaluation of three-terminal and four-terminal pair capacitors at high frequencies," *National Bureau of Standards Technical Note 1024*, 1980.

f) Free, G. M., Jones, R. N., "Calibration service for low-loss, three-terminal capacitance standards at 100 kHz and 1 MHz," *National Institute of Standards and Technology Technical Note 1348*, 1992.

g) Judish, R. M., Jones, R. N., "A generalized method for the calibration of four-terminal-pair type digital impedance meters," *National Bureau of Standards Interagency Report 84-3016*, 1984.

2.4 Rf/microwave power (thermistor detectors and power detectors)

2.4.1 Background

Power measurements (at the primary standards level) at microwave frequencies are usually done with calibrated thermistor detectors where the thermistor element is held at a constant resistance and the substituted dc power is used to indicate or calculate rf/microwave power input to the thermistor detector. Secondary power measurements can be done with a variety of detectors and configurations. Power detectors, other than thermistors, include thermoelectric and diode detectors, where the input power is related to an output voltage (usually after some amplification and conditioning). Power sensors of all kinds may be combined with directional couplers or attenuators to increase the power range.

2.4.2 Definitions

IEEE standard-IEEE 470-1972, *Application Guide for Bolometric Power Meters*, contains pertinent definitions for thermistor detectors and some additional definitions follow:

a) **Effective efficiency:** The ratio of the substituted dc power to the net rf/microwave input power to the power detector.

b) **Substituted dc power:** The dc power change in a self balancing bridge or power meter when rf/microwave power is applied to the power detector (with the thermistor held at its operating resistance, usually 100 or 200 Ω).

c) **Calibration factor:** Effective efficiency times $(1-|\Gamma|^2)$ where $|\Gamma|$ is the magnitude of the input reflection coefficient of the thermistor detector. Reflection coefficient is defined in 2.7.2.1.

2.4.3 Test and calibration methods and method validation

2.4.3.1 Most calibrations of thermistor detectors start by comparing a device under test (DUT) with a working standard thermistor detector. The working standard at NIST is usually measured in the NIST microcalorimeter although there are other ways of measuring the effective efficiency of a working standard. The working standard at any other level is simply a calibrated power detector (calibrated in the sense that the effective efficiency is known to some uncertainty). The DUT may be any of the aforementioned detectors.

2.4.3.2 The DUT is compared to the working standard using any of a variety of transfer techniques. A comprehensive, recent reference for power transfer techniques is Part C of Reference 2.4.5.2 a). Most transfer techniques deal with the elimination or reduction of mismatch errors in the calibration of a DUT. The mismatch errors exist because the working standard, the DUT, and the source to which they are connected have different reflection coefficients. The mismatch corrections are functions of the three complex reflection coefficients for the source generator, working standard, and DUT: Γ_g, Γ_{std}, and Γ_{DUT}, respectively, and are given in detail in the references.

a) The simplest technique is the direct comparison technique where the working standard and the DUT are each connected to the same source. This technique has a large uncertainty, unless the complex reflection coefficients of the source generator (Γ_g), working standard (Γ_{std}), and DUT (Γ_{DUT}) are known. The direct comparison technique includes thermistor/power meter-coupler transfer systems (see reference 2.4.5.2 a), Chapter 11 for complete discussion). The coupler may be replaced by a resistive power splitter. The detector-coupler system is simply a monitored source of CW power for which Γ_g is defined and can be measured. Reference 2.4.5.2 a), Chapter 11 has a list of references that give newer descriptions of techniques, although most of the older papers, references 2.4.5.2 h) and i) for example, still apply.

b) The tuned reflectometer technique essentially provides a matched source and the capability of measuring the magnitudes of Γ_{std} and Γ_{DUT}.

c) The 6-port technique applied to power calibration measures its own complex Γ_g and also the Γ_{std} for the working standard and Γ_{DUT} for the DUT.

2.4.4 Estimation of uncertainty of measurement

A complete analysis (source, magnitude and combining method) of uncertainties from the working standard through all the transfer techniques should be presented. The uncertainties should include, but not be limited to:

a) Working standard uncertainty,

b) How reflection coefficient mismatch factors are treated, and

c) Instrumentation uncertainties and dual element uncertainties in coaxial detectors.

2.4.5 References (measurement techniques)

2.4.5.1 IEEE standard 470-1972 includes recommended test methods and references (section 6) as of 1972.

2.4.5.2 A partial list of references for power meter calibration techniques follows: References a) - e) are the most recent sources for general power measurement techniques. Chapter 11 in a) is an especially comprehensive discussion of power meter transfer methods and uncertainties. Reference f) is a list of most of the power measurement publications as of 1967. One of the early papers on the direct comparison method is g) with mismatch considerations described in h) and the definition of generator reflection coefficient in i). Reference j) is the description of the tuned reflectometer technique, and k) and l) describe the application of "power equation" techniques. The use of a 6-port in power measurements is described in m). New papers describing the direct comparison method and the evaluation of the equivalent source mismatch term, n) and o), are now available.

a) Fantom, A., *Radio frequency and microwave power measurement*, Peter Peregrinus Ltd., London, U. K., 1990.

b) IEEE STD 470-72, *IEEE standard application guide for bolometric power meters*, Dec. 1972.

c) Hewlett-Packard, *Fundamentals of r.f. and microwave power measurements*, Appl. Note 64-1, Aug. 1977.

d) Hewlett-Packard, *Extended applications of automatic power meters*, Appl. Note 64-2, Sep. 1987.

e) Weinschel, Bruno O., Hancock, C. W., and Powell, R. C., "Techniques explained for CW power measurement," *Microwave Systems News & Communications Technology*, May 1986.

f) Rumfelt, A. Y., and Elwell, L. B., "Radio frequency power measurements," *Proc. IEEE.*, **55**, (6), pp. 837-850, Jun. 1967.

g) Desch, R. F., and Larson, R. E., "Bolometric microwave power calibration techniques at the National Bureau of Standards," *IEEE Trans. Instrum. Meas.*, **IM-12**, (1), pp. 2933, Jun. 1963.

h) Beatty, R. W., and Kerns, D. M., "Mismatch errors in microwave power measurements," *Proc. IRE*, **41**, pp. 1112-1119, Sep. 1953.

i) Engen, G. F., "Amplitude stabilization of a microwave signal source," *IRE Trans. on Microwave Theory and Tech.*, **MTT-6**, pp. 202-206, Apr. 1958.

j) Engen, G. F., "A transfer instrument for the intercomparison of microwave power meters," *IRE Trans. on Instrumentation*, **I-9**, pp. 202-208, Sep. 1960.

k) Hume, F. R., Koide, F. K., and Dederich, D. J., "Practical and precise means of microwave power meter calibration transfer," *IEEE Trans. Instrum. Meas.*, **IM-21**, (4), pp. 457-466, Nov. 1972.

l) Komarek, E. L., and Tryon, P. V., "An application of the power equation concept to precision bolometer unit calibration," *IEEE Trans. Microwave Theory Tech.*, **MTT-22**, (12), part II, pp. 1260-1267, Dec. 1974.

m) Engen, G. F., and Hoer, C. A., "Application of an arbitrary 6-port junction to power measurement problems," *IEEE Trans Instrum. Meas.*, **IM-21**, (4), pp. 470-474, Nov. 1972.

n) Weidman, M. P., "Direct Comparison Transfer of Microwave Power Sensor Calibrations," *NIST Technical Note 1379*, Jan. 1996.

o) Juroshek, J. R., "A Direct Calibration Method for Measuring Equivalent Source Mismatch," *Microwave Journal*, pp. 106-118, Oct. 1997.

2.5 Planar near-field range antenna calibration

2.5.1   Antenna test requirements

Accreditation will fall into three levels based on the difficulty of achieving the required uncertainties.

a) **Level 1** (the easiest level) will require a peak gain uncertainty of 0.5 dB or less, a sidelobe uncertainty of 5 dB or less at 25 dB below the far-field pattern peak, and a beam pointing determination uncertainty of 1 ° or less.

b) **Level 2** will require uncertainties of 0.3 dB or less for peak gain, 4 dB at sidelobes 40 dB below the far-field pattern peak, and 0.1 ° (or less) uncertainty for beam pointing determination.

c) **Level 3** will require uncertainties of 0.2 dB or less for peak gain, 5 dB at sidelobes 60 dB below the far-field pattern peak, and 0.01 ° (or less) uncertainty for beam pointing determination.

2.5.2   Range tests

2.5.2.1   For **level 1** accreditation, the magnitude of the following sources of uncertainty should be determined and their magnitudes consistent with level 1 uncertainty requirements (see references 2.5.7 a) and 2.5.7 b)):

a) Probe characterization,

b) Scanner alignment,

c) Scan-plane mirror alignment,

d) Test-antenna alignment,

e) Probe alignment,

f)   Rf-system dynamic range,

g)   Noise,

h)   Leakage,

i)   Probe test-antenna multiple reflections,

j)   Scan-plane truncation,

k)   System drift, and

l)   Insertion-loss amplitude and phase accuracies.

2.5.2.2   For **level 2** accreditation, all level 1 tests should be performed and the associated uncertainties limited in a way consistent with level 2 uncertainty requirements. In addition, the magnitudes of the following uncertainties should be determined and their magnitude appropriately limited (see references 2.5.7 a) and 2.5.7 b)):

a)   Probe-position errors,

b)   Rf-system linearity, and

c)   Aliasing.

2.5.2.3   For **level 3** accreditation, all level 1 and 2 tests should be performed and the magnitude of the associated uncertainties limited consistent with level 3 uncertainty requirements. In addition, the magnitude of the following uncertainties should be determined and the magnitude appropriately limited (see references 2.5.7 a) and 2.5.7 b)):

a)   Rf crosstalk between probe ports,

b)   Mixer ports,

c)   Coupler ports,

d)   Isolator ports and receiver channels,

e)   Amplitude and phase variation due to cable flexing,

f)   Multipath due to scattering from objects with the room, and

g)   Aliasing due to finite data-point spacing.

2.5.3   **Estimation of uncertainty of measurement**

Uncertainty budgets: Senior laboratory personnel should demonstrate the ability to determine the magnitude of various uncertainties and assemble an uncertainty budget for gain, for pattern, and for the determination of beam pointing, since uncertainties will be different for each probe test-antenna combination. References a) and b) in 2.5.7 below describe methods for determining uncertainties in planar near-field measurements.

2.5.4   Software comparison tests

To obtain far-field quantities, planar near-field measurement data require the processing of the data through correctly functioning software. To ensure that software is correctly functioning, the calibration laboratory needs to establish a standard data set that can be processed by laboratory software and compared to proven results to show that laboratory software is working correctly. Particular attention should be given to a consistent use of phase and time conventions.

2.5.5   Measurement traceability

For level 2 and level 3 accreditation, all near-field probes should be traceable to the National Institute of Standards and Technology in the calibration of their on-axis gain and polarization.

2.5.6   Measurement comparison

To ensure that overall uncertainty requirements can be met for level 2 and level 3 accreditation, a standard transfer antenna should be measured by the laboratory and results compared to those obtained by the accreditation agency. The standard antenna should have a pattern dynamic range consistent with the pattern accuracy requirements.

2.5.7   References

Descriptions of the range tests and the uncertainty-budget process can be found in the following references:

a)   Francis, M. H., Repjar, A. G., Kremer, D. P., "A certification plan for a planar near-field range used for high-performance phased-array testing," *Natl. Inst. Stand. Tech. Rep. NISTIR 3991*, 1992.

b)   Newell, A. C., "Error analysis techniques for planar near-field measurements," *IEEE Trans. Antenna Propagat.*, **AP-36**, pp. 754-768, June 1988.

2.6 Thermal noise calibration

2.6.1   Background

The determination of the noisiness of a circuit makes use of the rules for blackbody radiation, and the relationship between the radiated power spectral density and temperature. This is expressed as $P = kTB$ where P is the average power level, k is Boltzmann's constant, T is the circuit's equivalent blackbody temperature, and B is the circuit bandwidth. This means that an rf load at a known temperature can be used as the source for a known level of noise power. NIST's primary noise standards are built on this principle. The noise temperature of an unknown noise source is found by comparing its power spectral density with two standards having known noise temperatures. The calibration of such reference noise sources is the typical role of the calibration laboratory. On a more practical level, a calibrated noise source is used as a tool to find the so-called noise figure (NF) of a circuit having at least one input and output.

2.6.2   Definitions

2.6.2.1   Available power: The power that would be delivered into a conjugate matched load.

2.6.2.2 **Effective input noise temperature T_e:** The noise temperature of a source at the input of an ideal (zero noise) amplifier that would provide the same power spectral density at its output as one would get with a zero-Kelvin noise source attached to the real amplifier.

2.6.2.3 **Noise figure:** A measure of the amount of noise a device contributes to a system. This metric can be found by dividing the signal-to-noise ratio at the input of a device by the signal-to-noise ratio at its output when the input noise to the device is 290 K.

2.6.2.4 **Noise temperature:** The noise power spectral density divided by Boltzmann's constant. For a passive (one-port) device at physical temperature T_{phys}, the noise temperature is given by

$$T_n(f) = \frac{h\,f}{e^{\frac{hf}{kT_{phys}}} - 1} \qquad \text{(eq. 1)}$$

where f is the frequency and h is Planck's constant. Thus for low frequency and high temperature, the noise temperature of a passive one-port is approximately equal to its physical temperature. For active devices, there is no simple relationship between physical temperature and noise temperature.

2.6.2.5 **Y-factor:** The ratio of two different noise powers, typically

$$Y = \frac{P_{hot}}{P_{cold}}. \qquad \text{(eq. 2)}$$

For certain simplified conditions, this Y-factor is related to the noise temperatures of the two sources and the effective input noise temperature T_e,

$$Y = \frac{T_{hot} + T_e}{T_{cold} + T_e} \qquad \text{(eq. 3)}$$

Equation 3 is the basis of the "Y-factor method," in which T_e is determined by measuring Y.

2.6.3 **Accommodation and environmental conditions**

The ambient operating temperature range of the overall measurement system and standards should not vary more than 1 °C.

2.6.4 **Calibration methods**

2.6.4.1 Since the measurement system is designed to have a linear response, the noise measurement process typically uses two known noise standards to establish a calibrated power versus temperature curve for a high gain power detector. The unknown noise power is then compared against this calibration curve to find its effective noise temperature. This requires that the measurement system or radiometer have constant gain and be maintained with constant physical conditions (temperature, etc.). It is also important to account for any non-ideal (conjugate) rf impedance match between the sources being measured and the radiometer. The laboratory procedures used should account for or remove the effects of any test port impedance mismatch, and account for any measurement path difference for the noise standard and the device being tested.

2.6.4.2 The determination of a component's noise figure value is a modification of the techniques used to find the available noise power from a single port device. Basically, known noise sources are connected to the device's input port, and the noise power from the device is measured using a radiometer while varying the impedance of the noise standards connected.

2.6.5   References

a)   Daywitt, W. C., "Design and Error Analysis for the WR10 Thermal Noise Standard," *NBS Technical Note 1071*, 1984.

b)   Daywitt, W. C., "A Coaxial Noise Standard for the 1 GHz to 12.4 GHz Frequency Range," *NBS Technical Note 1074*, 1984.

c)   Wait, D. F., and G. F. Engen, "Application of Radiometry to the Accurate Measurement of Amplifier Noise," *IEEE Trans. on I&M*, **40**, (2), April 1991.

d)   Wait, D. F. and Randa, J., "Amplifier noise measurement at NIST," *IEEE Trans., Instrum. Meas.*, **IM-46**, pp. 482-485, 1997.

e)   Randa, J., "Uncertainties in NIST noise-temperature measurements," *NIST Tech. Note 1502*, 1998.

f)   Grosvenor, C., Randa, J., and Billinger, R. L., "Design and testing of NFRad – A new noise measurement system," *NIST Tech. Note 1518*, 2000.

2.7   Microwave measurements of scattering parameters

2.7.1   Background

Microwave signals are similar to light waves. The energy in a microwave signal is either reflected from or transmitted through a device. Microwave devices are characterized by measuring their reflection and transmission properties. Single port devices such as matched terminations and offset shorts are characterized by measuring their reflection properties or voltage reflection coefficient. Multiport devices such as attenuators and directional couplers are characterized by measuring both their reflection and transmission properties. These reflection and transmission properties are called scattering parameters or s-parameters. This section describes the technical requirements for making these types of microwave measurements.

2.7.2   Definitions

2.7.2.1 Voltage reflection coefficient: Voltage reflection coefficient is defined as the vector ratio of the reflected electric field relative to the incident electric field. The measurement is often referred to simply as reflection coefficient.

2.7.2.2 Scattering parameters (s-parameters):

a)   Scattering parameters relate the reflected and incident electric fields at each of the ports of a multiport device. The scattering parameters for a n-port device is given by a n x n matrix of complex numbers. That matrix is called the **scattering matrix** for the device. The voltage reflection coefficient is sometimes referred to as the **s-parameter of a 1-port device**.

b)   Other quantities can also be measured on microwave devices. However, those quantities can generally be shown to be related to the preceding basic measurements. Examples of some of these related measurements are:

1)   Attenuation;

2)   Phase shift;

3)   Impedance;

4)   Time delay;

5)   Group delay;

6)   Electrical length;

7)   Return loss;

8)   Insertion loss; and

9)   Substitution loss.

c)   Microwave measurements are generally phasor measurements that involve both the magnitude and phase of quantity being measured.

2.7.3   Test and calibration methods and method validation

2.7.3.1 Microwave measurements are normally made with either a vector or a scalar network analyzer. Most commercial, vector network analyzers are of the hetrodyne type where the signals of interest are converted to one or more intermediate frequencies prior to detection. Six-port vector network analyzers, in contrast, use coherent detection principles to make vector microwave measurements (see reference 2.7.6 f)).

2.7.3.2 A vector network analyzer measures both the magnitude and phase of the quantity of interest, while a scalar network analyzer measures only the magnitude of the quantity. Vector network analyzers are generally preferable to scalar network analyzers for precision measurements. Vector corrections can be made to a vector network analyzer to increase its accuracy. That process is usually referred to as calibration of the network analyzer.

2.7.3.3 In addition to network analyzers, other measurement techniques are used to measure attenuation (see reference 2.7.6. e)). Block diagrams for some of those techniques are shown in Figures 1 through 3.

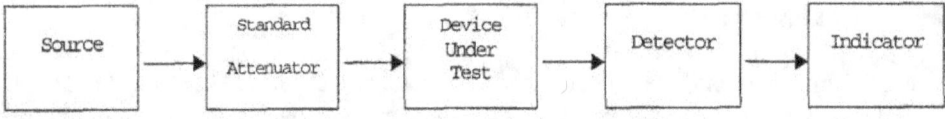

Figure 1. Attenuation measurement by rf substitution.

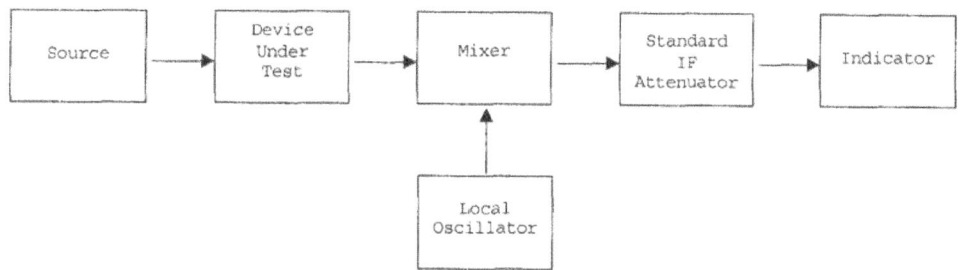

Figure 2. Attenuation measurement by IF substitution.

Figure 3. Attenuation measurement by audio or rf substitution.

2.7.3.4 Attenuation measurement by rf substitution relies on a standard attenuator for its measurements. The unknown device is simply compared to the standard attenuator to determine its attenuation. With this technique, the standard attenuator requires calibration at all measurement frequencies.

2.7.3.5 Attenuation measurement by intermediate frequency (IF) substitution is similar except the rf signal is translated to an IF prior to detection. Typical IF frequencies are 30 MHz or 1.25 MHz. With IF substitution, the standard attenuator requires calibration at only the IF frequency. The techniques shown in Figures 1 and 2 need not be limited to magnitude measurements. Coherent detectors can be used to provide both magnitude and phase information.

2.7.3.6 Attenuation measurement by audio or rf substitution uses a detector prior to the standard attenuator. This technique relies on the fact that low frequency attenuators can be calibrated to a high degree of accuracy. However, the detector nonlinearity has to be considered with this technique.

2.7.3.7 Slotted lines, and tuned reflectometers have also been used in the past for microwave measurements. However, these techniques are likely to be used only in those rare instances where conventional technology is not applicable.

2.7.4   Frequency range

The frequency range of microwave measurements is dependent on the type of connector that the device has. The frequency range for devices with coaxial connectors can range from dc to more than 110 GHz. The frequency range for devices with waveguide connectors is limited to an octave bandwidth that is dependent on the physical size of the waveguide.

2.7.5 Equipment

2.7.5.1 Microwave measuring systems rely on calibration standards for their accuracy. Calibration standards can generally be classified into one of the following five categories:

a)   Air lines,

b)   Fixed terminations,

c)   Sliding terminations,

d)   Offset or flat shorts and opens, and

e)   Standard attenuators.

2.7.5.2 With vector network analyzers, one or more calibration standards is connected to the system and measured. From these measurements, a set of error correction terms is generated. The error correction terms are then used to correct all subsequent measurements on that system. This error correction process is normally referred to as either "calibration" or "accuracy enhancement." Network analyzers are typically calibrated daily and the accuracy of their measurements can change significantly with each calibration. The accuracy of a network analyzer is highly dependent on the technique, care, condition, and quality of the connectors, cables, and calibration standards used.

2.7.5.3 With the systems shown in Figures 1 through 3, a "standard attenuator" is imbedded in the system. That attenuator is the standard to which all measurements are referenced. The accuracy of these systems tends to remain constant for longer periods of time. Standard attenuators require only periodic checks to assure that they remain within tolerance.

2.7.6 References

a)   IEEE Std. 474-1973, *IEEE Standard Specifications and Test Methods for Fixed and Variable Attenuators, DC to 40 GHz*, The Institute of Electrical and Electronic Engineers, New York, NY, 1973.

b)   ANSI/IEEE Std. 378-1986, *IEEE Standard on Network Analyzers (100 kHz to 18 GHz)*, The Institute of Electrical and Electronic Engineers, New York, NY, 1986.

c)   Somlo, P. I., and J. D. Hunter, *Microwave Impedance Measurements*, Peter Peregrinus Ltd., London, England, 1985.

d)   Kearns, D. M., and R. W. Beatty, *Basic theory of waveguide junctions and introductory microwave network analysis*, Pergamon Press, Oxford, England, 1967.

e)   Adams, S. F., *Microwave Theory and Applications*, Englewood Cliffs, NJ, 1969.

f)   Engen, G. F., *Microwave Circuit Theory and Foundations of Microwave Metrology*, Peter Peregrinus Ltd., London, England, 1992.

g)   MIL-C-39012C, *Military Specifications, Connectors, Coaxial, Radiofrequency*, U.S. Department of Defense.

h)   MIL-STD-45662A, *Calibration System Requirements*, U.S. Department of Defense, 1988.

i)	IEEE Std 287-1979, *IEEE Standard for Precision Coaxial Connectors*, The Institute of Electrical and Electronic Engineers, Inc., New York, NY, 1979.

j)	IEC Standard 457-3, *Rigid Precision Coaxial Lines and their Associated Precision Contacts, Parts 1 through 16*, Bureau Central de la Commission Electrotechnique Internationale, Geneva Switzerland.

k)	Estin, A. J., J. R. Juroshek, R. B. Marks, F. R. Clague, and J. Wayde Allen, "Basic rf and microwave measurements: a review of selected programs," *Metrologia*, **29**, 1992, pp 135-151.

l)	CIPM, BIPM Proc.-Verb. Com. Int. Poids et Mesures 49, 8-0, 26 (1981) (in French); P. Giacomo, "News from BIPM," *Metrologia* **18**, 41-44 (1982).

m)	CIPM, BIPM Proc.-Verb. Com. Int. Poids et Mesures 54, 14, 35 (1986) (in French); P. Giacomo, "News from the BIPM," *Metrologia* **24**, 45-51 (1987).

## 2.8	30-MHz attenuation calibration

### 2.8.1	Introduction

The accurate measurement of the attenuation of energy in coaxial and waveguide transmission lines is a fundamental requirement in the design, development, and operation of most electronic systems. Attenuators, which decrease rf energy in a precisely known way, should be calibrated by comparison with reference standards maintained by or traceable to the National Institute of Standards and Technology. For both technical and historical reasons, many rf, microwave, and millimeter wave measurements over the entire frequency spectrum are ultimately referenced to 30 MHz calibrations.

### 2.8.2	Definitions

2.8.2.1 Insertion loss: There are two definitions of insertion loss, one in which system mismatch is not specified, the other in which the system is nonreflecting. The definitions contradict each other since the insertion loss of an attenuator will be different for each case. The measurement procedure for both definitions is to open the system, insert the attenuator, and note the relative power absorbed by the load (or detecting device) before and after insertion. If the attenuator is variable and remains in the system, the initial and final powers absorbed by the load for two settings are used. This determination is more properly called "change of insertion loss." Either definition is entirely adequate for a single, unique system, but if the loss measurement is to be transferred from one laboratory to another, more should be specified about the system.

2.8.2.2 Attenuation: This is defined as the insertion loss in a nonreflecting system ($\Gamma_G = \Gamma_L = 0$, where Γ_G and Γ_L are defined as the reflection coefficients of the generator and load respectively). These impedance matching conditions cannot be achieved exactly because of imperfections in connectors and adapters, and the inability to ascertain when a system is precisely matched. Since attenuation cannot be measured exactly, the more practical term, "standard attenuation," has come into more general use.

2.8.2.3 Standard attenuation: This is defined as the insertion loss of a linear two-port device in an essentially nonreflecting system, which is initially connected together at the insertion point by a standard connector pair or waveguide joint. The nonreflecting condition is obtained in the standard coaxial or waveguide sections to which the standard connectors or waveguide joints are attached. The standard attenuation is the ratio expressed in dB of the power absorbed by the load before and after insertion of the two-port device being calibrated.

2.8.2.4 Incremental attenuation: Incremental attenuation is the change in attenuation of a variable attenuator between reference setting (usually zero) and any other setting. The same restraints on system conditions apply here as those for attenuation and standard attenuation. The term, "differential attenuation," is sometimes applied to this case and usually refers to two non-zero settings.

2.8.2.5 Decibel: The decibel, dB, is one tenth of a bel and is defined fundamentally in terms of a power ratio:

$$dB = 10 \, \log \left(\frac{P_1}{P_2} \right), \qquad\qquad (\text{eq. 4})$$

where P_1 is the incident power from an impedance matched source and P_2 is the net power into an impedance load after a device is inserted between the source and load. If powers P_1 and P_2 are associated with equal impedances, this power ratio can be expressed as the square of either the voltage or current ratio. Hence,

$$dB = 20 \, \log \left| \frac{V_1}{V_2} \right| = 20 \, \log \left| \frac{I_1}{I_2} \right|. \qquad\qquad (\text{eq. 5})$$

2.8.3   Equipment

2.8.3.1 A standard 30 MHz attenuator is a circular waveguide-below-cutoff (WBCO) attenuator with a continuously variable attenuation, commonly called a piston attenuator. The incremental attenuation of this type of standard can be accurately predicted from only a knowledge of the WBCO dimensions. Thus, a major advantage of this standard is the determination of the attenuation (except for secondary effects) from the fundamental units of length and time (frequency). When the waveguide section is uniform and excited in only one mode by a sinusoidal signal below the cutoff frequency, the field will decay exponentially along the guide.

2.8.3.2 The WBCO attenuator has a launching coil and a moving probe, or pick-up coil, to sample the decaying field and an indicating readout to correlate the probe position with the attenuation level change. The coupling coils in the attenuator should be sufficiently separated at all times to prevent mutual coupling and loading effects from excessively affecting the excited mode. This is the reason for high initial insertion loss of WBCO attenuators.

2.8.4   Test and calibration methods and method validation

2.8.4.1 Attenuation measurements are frequently performed below 1 GHz using intermediate frequency (IF) or audio frequency (AF) substitution techniques. These techniques have a number of sources of uncertainty since it is necessary to convert from one frequency to another. For this reason, they are not preferred and are not used at NIST. The direct substitution technique, whereby the standard attenuator and the attenuator under calibration operate at the same frequency, is a simpler approach with fewer sources of uncertainty.

2.8.4.2 An unmodulated two-channel system is employed at NIST. The two-channel nulled system has fewer problems of level instability in the source and gain stability of the monitor, and has high sensitivity. Phase and magnitude adjustments should both be made, so the system is more complex than a single channel system. A range of attenuation measurement in excess of 100 dB can be attained with this system by placing the device under test (DUT) in the insertion point in the magnitude channel. Quadrature detecting is used rather than a simple nulling approach so that better resolution can be maintained at small signal amplitudes.

To obtain a successful system, a precision phase shifter of constant amplitude or one with precisely known losses is required to achieve the quadrature phasing of the two channels.

2.8.4.3 When setting the attenuation level of many attenuators, care should be taken to remove the adverse effect of backlash in the drive mechanisms. The conventional procedure is always to approach the desired setting of the attenuator from a lower value of attenuator setting. This technique allows the very precise setting of the desired attenuation value.

2.8.5 Estimation of uncertainty of measurement

2.8.5.1 Uncertainties of a 30 MHz attenuation calibration system may divided into two groups, type A and type B. Type B uncertainties include:

a)   Resolution of the detecting system,

b)   Maximum rf leakage,

c)   Mismatch, and

d)   The reference standard piston attenuator.

2.8.5.2 Type A uncertainties depend on:

a)   The resettability and repeatability of the system, and

b)   The standard being measured.

2.8.6 Accommodation and environmental conditions

Care should be taken to ensure a stable environment. This includes parameters such as temperature, pressure, and humidity. A changing environment can cause system components to drift. Exactly how stable the environment should be controlled depends on the specific equipment used in the laboratory.

2.8.7 References

a)   Adair, R. T., Russell, D. H., "A Calibration Service for 30 MHz Attenuation and Phase Shift," *Natl. Inst. Stand. Technol. Special Publication 250-32* (1988).

b)   Russell, D. H., Larson, W., "RF Attenuation," *Proc. IEEE*, **55** (6), 942-959 (1967).

c)   Jargon, J. A., "A Revised Uncertainty Analysis for the NIST 30-MHz Attenuation Calibration System," *Proc. Meas. Sci. Conf.* (1994).

d)   Jargon, J. A., "A 30 MHz comparison receiver," *Asia-Pacific Microwave Conference Proceedings*, pp. 94-96, Taejon, Korea, Oct. 1995.

e)   Russell, D. H., "The waveguide below-cutoff attenuation standard," *IEEE Transactions on Microwave Theory and Techniques*, **45**, (12), pp. 2408-2413, 1997.

2.9 Rf-dc thermal voltage converter measurements

2.9.1. Introduction

This calibration service is designed, constructed and evaluated for the calibration of radio frequency voltage measuring devices and generators. The system covers a voltage range from 0.1 V to 300 V at frequencies from 30 kHz to 1 GHz. The standard developed to perform measurements in this region is the thermal voltage converter (TVC). Overall uncertainty of measurements vary from 0.05 % to 7.0 % (usually stated as μV/V) depending on the frequency, voltage level, and type of device being calibrated. The major system components, in addition to TVCs, are extremely stable rf sources, manual level controls, a precision direct current voltage source, and indicating circuits.

2.9.2. Applications of thermal voltage converters

TVCs are primarily used as rf voltage standards for the determination of rf voltage. Some of the more common applications are:

a)   Reference standards for the calibration of electronic rf voltmeters, rf voltage comparators, signal generators and field strength meters,

b)   Calibration of attenuators directly in terms of voltage ratios,

c)   Calibration of other reference standards such as attenuator-thermoelement voltmeters (ATVMs), other TVCs and rf micropotentiometers, and

d)   Calibration of power-measuring devices in terms of voltage and impedance.

2.9.3 Parameters measured

TVCs are used to calibrate numerous rf voltage-measuring devices and rf generators. The principle reference voltage is an rf voltage precisely measured at a specific reference plane. In addition, when values of voltages are compared with those from a dc source, the long-term stability characteristics of the laboratory voltage standards and the devices under test (DUTs) no longer affect the accuracy of the measurements. Therefore, only their short-term stabilities are significant when taking the difference between the rf and dc characteristics of the voltage standards. This inherent behavior greatly enhances the adaptability of these devices to the rf-dc difference technique of calibration.

2.9.4 Test and calibration methods and method validation

2.9.4.1 Several methods for the calibration of rf voltmeters utilize techniques that differ in principle of operation but are designed for the same goal. On an individual basis, there may be advantages with one technique, while another may provide a different benefit or benefits. Two different comparison procedures may be used.

2.9.4.2 In one type, the DUT is connected to a signal source and then the working standard is connected to measure the same alternating electrical quantity (current, voltage or power). The source is adjusted to produce the desired input of the DUT. Direct current is then applied to the standard and adjusted to reproduce its ac response, which is measured with the appropriate instrumentation. This is known as the "**straight ac test.**"

2.9.4.3 In the second method, both the standard and the DUT are connected to a source to simultaneously measure the quantity, first with ac and then with dc. In each case the applied quantity is adjusted to produce the same output indication of the DUT. The average is taken of the responses of the standard, of the forward and reverse polarity dc voltage applied at the same thermoelement-out voltage. This thermoelement voltage is the same as that measured when the rf signal is applied. From these average responses of the standard, the ac-dc difference of the DUT is computed. This is called the "**ac-dc difference test**."

2.9.5 Assuring the quality of test and calibration results

Measurement assessment is the combination of activities or process whose purpose is to provide assurance that the measurement system is accurate, repeatable and effective. It involves a continuous evaluation of performance of the calibration standards and system. To verify that the measurement process is in statistical control, additional standards such as check standards, are measured with the DUTs submitted for calibration. These check standards may be commercial TVCs similar to those DUTs normally calibrated and need not be of the quality of a national reference standard. Each check standard is calibrated directly with a working standard and measurements are incorporated in a database from which criteria for statistical control are established. Control charts are maintained for each of the check standards.

2.9.6 References

a) Selby, M. C., "Bolometric voltage and current (Bolovac) standard for high microwave frequencies," *Natl. Bur. Stand.(U.S.) J.Res.*, **72C**, (1), Jan-Mar 1968.

b) Hermach, F. L.and Williams, E. S., "Thermal voltage converters for accurate voltage measurements to 30 megacycles per second," *AIEE Trans. Pt. 1. Comm and Elec.*, July 1960.

c) Hermach, F. L., "An investigation of the uncertainties of the NBS thermal voltage and current converters," *Natl. Bur. Stand. (U.S.) NBSIR 84-2903*, April 1985.

d) Taylor, J. K., "Principles of quality assurance of chemical measurements," *Natl. Bur. Stand. NBSIR 85-3105*, Feb. 1985.

2.10 Rf-dc micropotentiometer measurements

2.10.1 Introduction

This calibration service is designed, constructed and evaluated for the calibration of radio frequency (rf) voltage measuring devices and generators. The system covers a voltage range from 1.0 mV to 200 mV at frequencies from dc to 1 GHz. The standard developed to perform measurements in this region is the rf micropotentiometer (μPOT). Overall uncertainty of measurement varies from 0.20 % to 2.0 % depending on the frequency, voltage level, and type of device being calibrated. The major system components, in addition to μPOTs, are extremely stable rf sources, manual level controls, a precision direct current voltage source and indicating circuits.

2.10.2 Applications of rf micropotentiometers

Rf μPOTS are primarily used as rf voltage standards for the determination of rf voltage. Some of the more common applications are:

a)   Reference standards for calibration of electronic rf voltmeters, rf voltage comparators, signal generators and field strength meters,

b)   Calibration of attenuators directly in terms of voltage ratios,

c)   Calibration of other reference standards such as thermal voltage converters (TVCs) and other rf micropotentiometers, and

d)   Calibration of power-measuring devices in terms of voltage and impedance.

2.10.3 Parameters measured

Rf micropotentiometers are used to calibrate numerous rf voltage-measuring and rf-generating devices. The principle reference voltage is an rf voltage precisely measured at a specific reference plane. In addition, when values of voltages are compared with those from a dc source, the long-term stability characteristics of the laboratory voltage standards and the devices under test (DUTs) no longer affect the accuracy of the measurements. Therefore, only their short-term stabilities are significant when taking the difference between the rf and dc characteristics of the voltage standards. This inherent behavior greatly enhances the adaptability of these devices to the rf-dc difference technique of calibration.

2.10.4 Test and calibration methods and method validation

2.10.4.1 Several methods for the calibration of rf measuring and generating devices (rf voltmeters, signal sources) use techniques that differ in principle of operation but are designed for the same goal. On an individual basis, there may be advantages with one technique, while another may provide a different benefit or benefits.

2.10.4.2 Suitable devices for primary measurements of rf voltage include:

a)   Thermistor mounts with associated dc bridge circuits,

b)   Measurement of current through a known resistance, and

c)   Precision rf voltmeters.

2.10.4.3 In addition, with the rf micropotentiometer, a dc voltage is substituted for a known rf voltage all applied at a specific voltage reference plane. Two different comparison procedures may be used.

a)   In one type, the DUT is connected to a signal rf source to measure both the standard and the unknown. The electrical quantity that is measured is the dc voltage output of the μPOT. The output of the source and the working standard is connected to measure the same output (it is assumed that the output does not change). The source is adjusted to produce the desired reflection of the DUT. Direct current is then applied to the standard and adjusted to reproduce its ac response, which is measured with the appropriate instrumentation. This is known as the **"straight ac test."**

b)   In the second method, both the standard and the DUT are connected to a source to simultaneously measure the output, first with rf and then with dc. In each case the applied quantity is adjusted to produce the same output indication of the DUT. The average is taken of the responses of the standard, and from this the ac-dc difference of the DUT is computed. This is called the **"ac-dc difference test."**

2.10.4.4 In both of these tests, the substitution of a direct for an alternating quantity is performed. This is called **"direct substitution."** Another type of voltage measurement employs the basic entity of temperature as the medium of transfer. In this case, the emf produced by a thermopile heated with rf power is compared with the emf produced by the same thermopile with dc power.

2.10.5 Assuring the quality of test and calibration results

Measurement assessment is the combination of activities or process whose purpose is to provide assurance that the measurement system is accurate, repeatable and effective. It involves a continuous evaluation of performance of the calibration standards and system. To verify that the measurement process is in statistical control, additional standards such as check standards, are measured with the DUTs submitted for calibration. These check standards may be commercial µPOTs similar to those DUTs normally calibrated and need not be of the quality of a national reference standard. Each check standard is calibrated directly with a working standard and measurements are incorporated in a database from which criteria for statistical control are established. Control charts are maintained for each of the check standards.

2.10.6 References

a)   Selby, M. C., "Bolometric voltage and current (Bolovac) standard for high microwave frequencies," *Natl. Bur. Stand. (U.S.) J.Res.*, **72C**, (1), Jan-Mar 1968.

b)   Hermach, F. L. and Williams, E. S., "Thermal voltage converters for accurate voltage measurements to 30 megacycles per second," *AIEE Trans., Pt. 1. Comm and Elec.*, July 1960.

c)   Hermach, F. L., "An investigation of the uncertainties of the NBS thermal voltage and current converters," *Natl. Bur. Stand. (U.S.) NBSIR 84-2903*, April 1985.

d)   Taylor, J. K., "Principles of quality assurance of chemical measurements," *Natl. Bur. Stand. NBSIR 85-3105*, Feb. 1985.